May 2018

WORKING IN
SCIENCE

by Lisa Idzikowski

www.12StoryLibrary.com

12-Story Library is an imprint of Bookstaves and Press Room Editions

Produced for 12-Story Library by Red Line Editorial

Photographs ©: mediaphotos/iStockphoto, cover, 1; BeyondImages/iStockphoto, 4; Monkey Business Images/Shutterstock Images, 5, 21, 27, 28; all_about_people/Shutterstock Images, 6; Steve Debenport/iStockphoto, 7; Kirsanov Valeriy Vladimirovich/Shutterstock Images, 8; ziggy_mars/ Shutterstock Images, 9; wavebreakmedia/Shutterstock Images, 10; vaalaa/Shutterstock Images, 11; fotografixx/iStockphoto, 12; Ugreen/iStockphoto, 13; Alexander Kolomietz/Shutterstock Images, 14, 29; Photodiem/Shutterstock Images, 15; goodluz/Shutterstock Images, 16; PhilAugustavo/iStockphoto, 17; Lavinia Bordea/Shutterstock Images, 18; Jennifer Heldmann/National Science Foundation, 19; NASA, 20; Kevin L Chesson/Shutterstock Images, 22; frank_peters/Shutterstock Images, 23; Allexxandar/Shutterstock Images, 24; KSC/NASA, 25; Production Perig/Shutterstock Images, 26

Library of Congress Cataloging-in-Publication Data
Names: Idzikowski, Lisa, author.
Title: Working in science / by Lisa Idzikowski.
Description: Mankato, MN : 12 Story Library, [2017] | Series: Career files |
   Audience: Grades 4 to 6. | Includes bibliographical references and index.
Identifiers: LCCN 2016047452 (print) | LCCN 2016051009 (ebook) | ISBN
   9781632354488 (hardcover : alk. paper) | ISBN 9781632355157 (pbk. : alk.
   paper) | ISBN 9781621435679 (hosted e-book)
Subjects: LCSH: Science--Vocational guidance--Juvenile literature.
Classification: LCC Q147 .I39 2017 (print) | LCC Q147 (ebook) | DDC
   502.3--dc23
LC record available at https://lccn.loc.gov/2016047452

Printed in the United States of America
022017

Table of Contents

Science Has an Amazing Variety of Careers

Imagine discovering a medicine that could cure cancer. Picture yourself battling rain and strong winds to study hurricanes. Consider how you might find evidence at a crime scene. All these jobs have a few things in common. They can be fun, exciting, and important. And they all involve science.

Some scientists get up close and personal with natural disasters.

Science is the process of learning things based on research and evidence. The number of scientific fields is vast. People study life, Earth, space, chemistry, physics, and many other subjects. Scientists use their knowledge to make predictions, perform experiments, and analyze the results. This process has made our modern world possible. Today, people in scientific careers continue learning about the universe and improving lives.

7

Percentage increase expected in US scientific jobs between 2015 and 2024.

- Now is a good time to think about a career in science.
- Science jobs are a growing part of the workforce.
- With so many different scientific fields, there is an area of interest for everyone.

Scientists use cutting-edge technology to make amazing advances.

Getting Started in Science

How can students decide if a science career is right for them? Many students are excited to make or discover things. Some watch birds or collect rocks and minerals. Others observe thunderstorms or grow vegetables in a school garden. These types of activities might be a clue that science is a great career choice.

Scientists like challenges. They solve problems in creative ways. Learning about their chosen fields is important. But employers want workers with other key skills, too.

Future scientists should learn to use computers. They should pay attention to details, and they should be good organizers. They should also practice communication skills. They will need to be able to share their research with others.

Preparing for a scientific career can start as early as elementary school. Math and science classes can give students early ideas of their interests. At the same time, classes in computers, English, and other subjects will help them practice important skills.

In high school, students can continue studying science and math. They can participate in activities such as robotics clubs and science fairs. They can explore free online classes in programming and other subjects. As they advance toward graduation, students

Birdwatching is a great hobby for people interested in science.

Students can practice building drones and other devices in after-school clubs.

should consider what kinds of careers interest them.

Almost all science careers require education after high school. Some students earn associate's degrees. These usually involve two years of study. Graduates with associate's

degrees can work as technicians in scientific labs. They help scientists carry out experiments.

Other students earn bachelor's degrees. These usually require four years of study. Students choose a field that interests them, such as biology, geology, or physics. They take many classes on their chosen subject. Graduates with bachelor's degrees have more career options than those with associate's degrees.

For some science careers, even more schooling is needed. Students can continue their education and earn master's degrees or doctorate degrees. With these advanced degrees, they can design new research projects and run laboratories. They can also get jobs as university professors.

$62,160

The average annual salary for scientific careers in 2015, according to the Bureau of Labor Statistics.

- Young people should find out what they are excited to learn.
- Almost all scientific careers require some college education.
- People who earn more advanced degrees usually have more career options.

Entomologists Are Studying Bugs

Bees, butterflies, beetles, and many other insects live in the world around us. Entomologists study these fascinating creatures. Some explore life cycles and behavior. Others discover the effects insects have on people, other animals, and plants. These scientists work outside, in labs, and at universities. They use computers, microscopes, and other tools.

Some insects, such as bees, are helpful to people. Bees pollinate food crops. They help the plants grow. Entomologists track bee populations. They make sure bees stay healthy. Healthy bees mean healthy crops.

Some insects are harmful to people. Mosquitoes carry dangerous diseases. They transmit malaria and

Entomologists sometimes wear head lamps to study bugs at night.

the Zika virus. Entomologists find ways to limit the spread of these insects. This helps keep disease rates down.

People interested in entomology sometimes collect insects that live near them. They study insect field guides and check out local museums to learn more. Students interested in entomology careers may earn degrees in wildlife biology or zoology. The creatures entomologists study may be tiny, but insects play a big role in our world.

Collecting insects is often done with a net.

8,000

Approximate number of people in entomology careers in the United States.

- Entomologists study insects.
- Entomologists often earn college degrees in wildlife biology or zoology.
- Students can get a start by observing insects in their own backyards.

VOLUNTEER ENTOMOLOGISTS

Even without a college degree, people can participate in entomology. Volunteers all over the United States and Canada are helping scientists with projects. One project aims to learn about monarch butterfly migration. Volunteers tag butterflies with identification stickers. This lets scientists track the monarchs' movements.

Scientists Are Making Plants Better

Plant scientists improve the world's crops. Some of these scientists study why some food crops fail and others flourish. They share what they learn with farmers. Others develop crops that grow in harsh conditions. They make it possible to grow food in more places. Plant scientists work for private businesses, in government offices, and at university labs.

Soil may sound like a boring topic. But for many scientists, it is the key to improving the world. Soil scientists analyze the ground in which crops are planted. They measure moisture and nutrients. They examine insects. Sometimes they take samples. Other times

In cold regions, plants can be studied year-round in greenhouses.

70,000

Number of different types of soil in the United States.

- Plant scientists study why plants grow well in certain conditions.
- Soil scientists explore how soil conditions affect plants.
- Home gardens give people a chance to experiment with plants and soil in their own backyards.

PLANTS IN SPACE

Plants provide food for people on Earth, but what about astronauts? Some plant scientists are working to develop crops that can grow in space. Besides providing food for astronauts, these plants could also create oxygen to breathe.

they study the soil using satellite photos. They ensure that crops are productive and sustainable.

Building a home garden is a great way to learn about plants and soil. Students who want to turn this hobby into a career should enroll in a university. Classes on biology, plant diseases, and entomology can lead to a career in plant science.

Studying crops from the sky or space can give scientists a broader view of how the plants are doing.

Biochemists Explore Life's Chemistry

Biochemists explore the chemical makeup of living things. They have the opportunity to save or improve people's lives. These scientists develop better tests for detecting disease. They create new medicines to treat illnesses.

To accomplish these things, biochemists investigate chemical reactions in the body. They watch what happens during processes such as aging, breathing, and digestion. They work in labs and offices and perform experiments. Then they share results with other scientists. Lasers, special microscopes, x-ray machines, computers, and other equipment make their work possible.

Biochemists often work in high-tech labs.

Over decades of research, biochemists have discovered the parts of human cells and how they work.

Biologists look at whole creatures. Biochemists look at cells, the tiny parts that make up those creatures. Each person is made of a vast number of cells. And each cell is constantly abuzz with activity. Learning how cells work and work together is the tough task of biochemists. Scientists have made great advances in this field, but there is still much to discover.

37.2 trillion
Approximate number of cells in a human body.

- Biochemists study the chemical processes in living organisms.
- Many technological tools, including computers and special microscopes, are used in biochemistry.
- Biochemists play a role in detecting and fighting diseases.

THINK ABOUT IT

Two key subjects for biochemistry students are chemistry and computers. Why might this combination of skills be so important for this career?

Farming with Science and Technology

Agricultural technicians perform many tasks in the farming industry. Some collect and test samples of food, animal products, or seeds. Others maintain and repair high-tech farm equipment. They may also conduct experiments. They work in labs, farms, greenhouses, or offices.

The world's population increases each year. All those people need food. By helping farms run smoothly, agricultural technicians make sure enough food is grown.

Some recent high school graduates can jump into this career. They train

Using drones to study crops is one way to combine agriculture and technology.

with an experienced technician and learn on the job. They may enroll in a two-year associate's degree program for crop or animal science, too. Agricultural technology is a great career for those enjoy science, hands-on work, and farming.

Junior technicians can train with experienced ones to advance their careers.

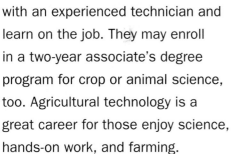

2.07 million

The approximate number of farms in the United States in 2015.

- Agricultural technicians do many tasks in the farming industry.
- Agricultural technicians work in a wide variety of locations.
- People can enter agricultural technician careers soon after high school.

Hydrologists Watch the Water

Hydrologists help ensure that communities have safe, clean water.

Hydrologists keep a watch on the water supply. They collect samples and test them for pollution. If unsafe water is discovered, scientists find ways to combat the contamination. They also prepare for water-related disasters. They can warn communities about floods or water shortages. Many are also hired to supervise the placement and drilling of water wells.

Besides working in labs and offices, hydrologists spend many hours out in the country. They use computers and satellites to find their way in remote locations. High-tech devices let them collect, analyze, and report data.

Students interested in hydrology can choose a university that offers an Earth science program. They should also practice communication, critical thinking, and teamwork. These skills will help them in their future career. Most water scientists continue with

WARNING
POLLUTED WATER
Unsafe for Drinking or Recreational Use

DIRECTOR OF PUBLIC HEALTH
DEPARTMENT OF PUBLIC HEALTH

Scientists in the hydrology field may communicate with governments to keep citizens well informed.

schooling until they earn a master's degree. Some working hydrologists travel to other countries. For this reason, learning another language can be helpful, too.

Fresh, safe water is a priceless resource. Hydrologists help protect it. Their work will always be needed to create a safe, healthy world.

355 billion

Estimated number of gallons (134 billion L) of water per day used by the United States in 2010.

- Hydrologists study water.
- Hydrologists help ensure water is safe for people to use.
- Hydrology careers often require schooling beyond four years of college.

17

Charting Climate and Weather

Atmospheric scientists investigate and measure the conditions of the atmosphere. Some explore weather. Others learn about the climate. The weather involves short-term events in the atmosphere. The climate involves the average weather conditions over a long period of time.

One common task for meteorologists is predicting the weather. They put together information from a worldwide network of weather observations. This data comes from thermometers, barometers, radar, satellites, and weather balloons. Some meteorologists work for television stations. They share their forecasts with viewers each day.

Climate scientists track the changes in the climate over many years. Data from the last few hundred years has been recorded by people. But scientists can also learn what the climate was like in earlier times.

Weather stations collect data and send it to meteorologists around the globe.

800,000

Number of years of the climate record that some ice core samples show.

- Atmospheric scientists study weather and climate.
- Meteorologists forecast the weather, the conditions over a short period of time.
- Climate scientists learn about the climate, the conditions over a long period of time.

STORM CHASERS

Some meteorologists get close to storms to study them. They are called storm chasers. They may wait hours for a tornado to form. They don't always know what they will encounter. Sometimes they find hailstones larger than baseballs. Sometimes they face roaring winds or pounding rain. Their job is dangerous but important.

They drill into polar ice to collect samples. The samples look like long cylinders. Each ice sample, called a core, contains many layers. These layers were created at different times. Some go back thousands of years. Scientists can study the layers to learn what the climate was once like.

Simple weather tracking can be done at home with a thermometer. Volunteers across the country collect local weather data. This helps scientists develop a more complete picture of the nation's weather.

A NASA researcher drills an ice core in Antarctica.

Food Scientists Are Testing and Tasting

Food scientists develop processed foods and food containers. They work in laboratories to create new flavors. They find ways to make foods healthier and tastier. And they test foods to ensure they are safe for consumers.

Many items on supermarket shelves are the result of research by food scientists. They study the chemistry of food. They also explore the science of how the human body tastes and digests food. Well-designed containers and packaging make sure the food stays fresh.

Without food scientists, food might go bad on the way to the store or on store shelves. Consumers would not know the nutritional content of their foods. They would risk getting

The workspace of a food scientist may be part laboratory, part kitchen.

sick every time they bought food from the store. Food would also lack the flavors that many people enjoy. The world of food would look vastly different without the work of these dedicated scientists.

1.2 million

The number of places, including restaurants and stores, that sell food in the United States.

- Food scientists develop foods and food containers.
- Food scientists explore the chemistry of food.
- Food scientists play important roles in keeping consumers healthy.

Food scientists have made the wide variety of products in modern grocery stores possible.

Forensic Scientists Are Solving Crimes

Forensic scientists are members of crime solving teams. They find evidence to help identify and catch criminals. Their work helps police and courts do their jobs.

Some forensic scientists work at crime scenes. They find evidence. This may include bullet casings, drops of blood, and tiny threads of fabric. They also photograph or sketch the overall crime scene. This helps them figure out how each piece of evidence fits together.

Forensic scientists work at laboratories, too. They study the evidence under microscopes. They match crime scene fingerprints with police records. They check victims' bodies for drugs or poisons. Forensic scientists figure out what happened at the crime scene. They may be called to appear in court and share their findings.

Other forensic scientists work with computers. They track crimes committed online. They find evidence on computer hard drives.

Some universities have four-year programs designed especially for forensic science. Others teach

Forensic scientists use high-tech tools to study evidence left at crime scenes.

1902

The year that US forensic scientists began using fingerprint identification.

- Forensic scientists find and study evidence at crime scenes.
- Some forensic scientists deal with crimes committed on computers.
- People who pay attention to detail find this career a good fit.

COMPUTER FORENSICS

Forensic science is a booming career. As technology improves, criminals are finding more ways to commit crimes using computers. Hacking, identity theft, and other illegal activities are becoming more common. Skilled computer forensics experts will be needed to catch these criminals.

individual courses in related subjects. Whichever path students take, they must work to sharpen several skills. Problem solving and attention to detail are key. So are computer and communication skills.

Increases in computer-related crimes have resulted in a need for more forensic scientists with computer expertise.

Planetary Scientists Explore the Universe

Planetary scientists study Earth and the other planets. Sometimes they explore space through telescopes. Other times, they send spacecraft to these worlds. They use their observations to form new theories about the universe.

These scientists work closely with experts in other fields. Engineers design the rockets and spacecraft they use. Geologists study the landscapes of the moon. Atmospheric scientists study the whirling clouds of Jupiter and Saturn. And biologists explore whether life might exist on Mars.

People can use simple backyard telescopes to begin learning about our solar system.

Today's planetary scientists are at the cutting edge of technology. Spacecraft with advanced sensors and cameras have reached the outer limits of our solar system. They beam back data over billions of miles.

Planetary scientists must be dedicated to their work. A space mission may take years to complete. The *New Horizons* spacecraft launched from Earth in 2006. It finally reached its destination, Pluto, in 2015.

A group of scientists stands in front of the rocket that later launched *New Horizons* to Pluto.

4.67 billion

Furthest approximate distance, in miles (7.5 billion km), from Earth to Pluto.

- Planetary scientists study Earth and other planets.
- Planetary scientists work alongside experts in many other fields.
- The work of planetary scientists may take many years to complete.

THINK ABOUT IT

What kinds of things do you think planetary scientists can learn using telescopes? What additional things can they learn by sending spacecraft to planets?

Scientists Are Discovering the Future

Discoveries and inventions will change, but the basic ideas of science remain the same. Scientists observe the world around them. They make predictions about how the world works. Then they design experiments to test these guesses. Over time, this process adds new knowledge to the world.

Scientists are making progress in many fields. Some make life-saving medicines. Others grow plentiful, healthy food. Some examine the tiny cells that make up our bodies. And others explore the furthest parts of our solar system.

Tomorrow's scientists will continue to work not just in laboratories, but also out in the field.

Today's students will be tomorrow's leading scientists. Each career area will need many dedicated, hard-working people. Through careful study, they will help make the world a better place.

97,600

The estimated number of new science jobs that will be added in the United States between 2014 and 2024.

- The process of science is constantly adding new knowledge to the world.
- Science touches every part of people's lives.
- Today's students will become the pioneering scientists of tomorrow.

Science classrooms across the globe are inspiring the next generation of scientific innovators.

Other Jobs to Consider

Astronomer

Description: Work to understand stars, galaxies, and other objects in space, such as black holes
Training/Education: Doctorate degree for most jobs
Outlook: Estimated 7 percent increase in jobs from 2014 to 2024
Average salary in 2015: $110,980

Biological Technician

Description: Assist biologists with research, testing, and the manufacturing of new products
Training/Education: Associate's degree in science technology or a bachelor's degree in biology or chemistry
Outlook: Estimated 5 percent increase in jobs from 2014 to 2024
Average salary in 2015: $41,650

Environmental Science and Protection Technician

Description: Work to keep the environment and people safe from pollution

Training/Education: Associate's degree, and for some jobs a bachelor's degree

Outlook: Estimated 9 percent increase in jobs from 2014 to 2024

Average salary in 2015: $43,030

Geoscientist

Description: Study Earth and its natural resources, including water, rocks and minerals, and oil

Training/Education: Master's degree for most jobs

Outlook: Estimated 10 percent increase in jobs from 2014 to 2024

Average salary in 2015: $89,700

Glossary

agricultural
Having to do with farming.

contamination
The process of making a substance unsafe by adding something harmful.

forecasts
Predictions of what will happen in the future.

migration
The act of moving from one place to another.

pollinate
To move pollen from one plant to another, helping the plants reproduce.

research
To carefully study or investigate a certain subject in order to discover or explain new knowledge.

sustainable
Able to be used without destroying natural resources.

technician
A person skilled in the techniques of science.

For More Information

Books

Carmichael, L. E. *Discover Forensic Science*. Minneapolis, MN: Lerner Publications, 2017.

Hamen, Susan E. *Astronomy in the Real World*. Minneapolis, MN: Abdo Publishing, 2016.

Mangor, Jodie. *Women in Physical Science*. Minneapolis, MN: Abdo Publishing, 2016.

Visit 12StoryLibrary.com

Scan the code or use your school's login at **12StoryLibrary.com** for recent updates about this topic and a full digital version of this book. Enjoy free access to:

- Digital ebook
- Breaking news updates
- Live content feeds
- Videos, interactive maps, and graphics
- Additional web resources

Note to educators: Visit 12StoryLibrary.com/register to sign up for free premium website access. Enjoy live content plus a full digital version of every 12-Story Library book you own for every student at your school.

Index

About the Author

Lisa Idzikowski is a writer and former science teacher from Milwaukee, Wisconsin. She loves science, history, and living near Lake Michigan. When she isn't reading, researching, or writing, Lisa works on her native plant garden to attract birds, bees, and butterflies.

READ MORE FROM 12-STORY LIBRARY

Every 12-Story Library book is available in many formats. For more information, visit 12StoryLibrary.com.